How to Flirt and be Seductive

D1634716

This book is dedicated to
my grandmother Peta, who was
the most seductive woman
I have known.
And to my daughter,
Vassilissa, who has yet
to become one

CONTENTS

How to Flirt and be Seductive

Valentina Artsrunik

ARTNIK • LONDON

First published in Great Britain in 2003
by Artnik
341b Queenstown Road
London SW8 4LH UK

This is a revised edition of an earlier book, *How to Flirt and be Seductive* 2001

ISBN 1 903906 02 4

Illustrations: Geoff Searle
Printed and bound in Spain by Bookprint

and try to appease deep insecurities, we
are polygamous.

The ability to reconcile this dichotomy
and find an inner balance is a sign of
maturity that many never attain. Most
of us are perpetually stuck in a mind-set
of old preconceptions, social taboos, and
traditional and religious dictates.

Some still rebel but most of them become
prisoners of their rebellion and strive to
fit the image, rather than live with a measure
of happiness.

Perhaps, rather than agonise over age-old
questions to which we may never have
the true answer, we should heed the advice
of Dionysus who advocated the simple
pleasures found in a goblet of wine and
anguish-free merriment.

FINAL WORDS
OF WISDOM

Seduce and allow yourself
to be seduced –
this is the staff of life.

Those who do not play a seductive
'game' are the most seductive.

INTRODUCTION

*Flirting is one of the most delightful
and wickedly addictive games
of all time.*

Imagine the scene. A room full of people.
A woman sits in one corner of it, holding
a glass in her hand. A man catches her eye
from the other end of the room.

She does not stare – that would be impolite
– but she has registered the attention and
will, from this moment on, frequently divert
her eyes in his direction.

She is talking to other people, but her smile is destined for the man at the other end of the room.

He knows it and acknowledges this by lifting his glass in a silent toast. The woman moves her hair – she tosses it back or plays with a strand.

She strokes her forearm, crosses and uncrosses her legs, pouts slightly, arches her eyebrows.

When she gets up and walks her hips sway and her shoulders straighten up to show her bosom to its best advantage.

She moves feline-like across the room as the man watches and times his approach.

There is magnetism and a raw sensual power that passes a current between them.

Some call it chemistry.
I call it magic.

The art of flirting and the ritual of seduction have developed in response to the most powerful, compulsive and primeval urge in man – mating and reproduction.

As with every ritual, decorum and rules have evolved over the ages, but the pursuit of love and/or sex has remained a basic and essential preoccupation of men and women alike.

From the tribal mating dance to the most sophisticated game of seduction there always emerges a victor, and he or she is the one who understands best how to generate excitement – the excitement of the chase – and who appreciates what constitutes real gratification.

This guide aims to explore what makes certain people stand out for their charm and power of seduction, how they do it, and how each and every one of us can discover the inner resources to captivate the object of our desire.

In an ever-changing world, certain things remain unaltered – physical attraction, infatuation, love, obsession, envy, jealousy, passion...

These driving forces are second to none in what makes us happy or unhappy.

To understand and to harness them is to play with a winning hand in what most of us think is a game of chance.

HISTORICAL PERSPECTIVES

The most primitive and ancient act of seduction took the form of the male waging a contest for the female. It is still acted out – in one manner or another – even though the proponents of political correctness like to pretend otherwise.

That the female often provokes such contests is not in dispute.

While the primitive male used spears,
and later swords, to demonstrate
chivalry and win the heart of the

woman of his choice, the contemporary man resorts to wit, sense of humour, a fancy car or a large wallet, career prospects, stock portfolio and so on.

However, courage — whether physical or spiritual — cannot be discounted even today and most women are programmed to respond to a demonstration of strength, especially when it is played out for their benefit.

Primitive females used body language and adornments to entice the male.

One needs only to examine the evolution of fashion to come to the conclusion that political correctness has done nothing to alter this — hence the rising hem, the plunging neckline and the fancy footwear,

not to mention a whole industry devoted
to undergarments.

Meanwhile, body painting and tribal dancing
have been replaced by make-up, hair-colour-
enhancing treatments and...dancing.

Look at the crowds in a discotheque.
With their rhythm, body gyrations,
noise and palpable sexuality, don't
they remind you of the original
tribal dancers?

The revival of the tango and the
popularity of the salsa bear testimony to
the power of dance and body language
as a means to seduction.

To begin with, man was the provider and
protector, while the woman was the child bearer.

The human race has made it this far because
men chose mates with the best child-rearing
prospects and women went with the victors
of raw strength and bravery contests.

So the survival of the fittest weeded out

weaklings and improved the human species. There is no doubt that things have become rather more complicated since.

While a voluptuous figure signified fertility in past centuries, a skeletal body is what is greatly prized today.

Or is it?

Magazines are full of pictures of pouting beanstalk-like models with hollow cheeks. But our inbred sense of what is aesthetically pleasing and healthy inevitably directs us to lust after the fuller figure.

Thus, Marilyn Monroe became the ultimate sex symbol of all time. She might not make it to the pages of today's fashion magazines, but there isn't a man who hasn't had a secret fantasy about her at one time or another.

Women may have careers now and postpone childbearing until much later in life, but they are still genetically programmed to strive for motherhood.

Their very independence from men has created frustrations associated with their inability to find a mate with whom they can fulfil this basic need.

The modern man, meanwhile, exists in a maelstrom of confusion.

His own genetic programming dictates that he takes the driving seat in a monogamous relationship, but if he so much as hints at such intent he is lambasted by self-appointed spokespersons of women's liberation.

And so, what we have now is a complicated maze of our own ideological making.

The more we try to figure a way out of it, the more lost we become.

In response volumes have been written on the subject of male-female relationships — how we are different and why, and how we can overcome these differences and understand one another.

But the truth is that we were never meant to overcome our differences any more than we were intended to understand them.
man and woman merely accepted them and used them to their advantage, with the ultimate aim of simply seducing one another.

FLIRTING AS A BIOLOGICAL IMPERATIVE

Flirting begins as soon as hormones start kicking in.

Thus, we observe the early fascination that girls and boys have with each other even before they know why they have it.

At the age of exploration flirting is at its most guileless and without artifice — it is natural and motivated purely by biological imperative rather than by the excitement of 'the game'.

Girls and boys of the same chronological age have a different sexual age, but both sexes react to fairly basic impulses pre-determined by gender and sexual inclination.

Flirtation, however clumsy, is an expression of a young boy's physiological imperatives; young girls perceive flirtation as a means of getting attention and fulfilling certain romantic dreams.

But both boys and girls develop an intense fascination with each other that lasts a lifetime and perpetually veers between comprehension and bewilderment.

Almost instinctively, teenage girls become aware of the attentions of older males. They can be flattered or repulsed by them, but they never fail to react strongly. A sub-conscious reaction — a testing of their power as it were — is the very provocative and often tasteless way in which they sometimes dress.

Tantalising an older male, however innocently engaged in by the girl, can lead her into serious trouble.

For while boys accept teasing as part
of the ritual, grown-up men can be
tempted into carrying the flirtation to
its natural conclusion.

Is there a girl who hasn't been groped on
a crowded bus, accosted with some lewd
comment or other, or made to suffer the

heaving of an aroused dancing partner whose age is closer to her father's than it is to hers!

Older men woo girls more thoughtfully than do younger boys (who tend to take them for granted).

Younger boys assume that girls experience the same physiological sense of urgency and that they prolong flirtation out of sheer mischief – playing hard to get as it were.

While many girls do play that game because they have been led to believe that it is the most alluring way to behave and to bewitch a man, many have no desire to yield to sexual advances.

It is girls' intense curiosity, fuelled by teen novels and peer pressure to appear more mature and worldly, that makes them yield to seduction.

As girls turn into women and boys into men, the former become more adept at seduction and the latter more selective.

Men become selective because they are conditioned to carry the financial burden of a family. If they have not yet found a mate, women in their thirties and early forties may abandon discrimination.

As their reproductive life nears an end, flirtation can turn desperate.

When they have been married and produced children, women become more discerning with age. They may flirt out of habit, but they flirt with deeper motives if they consider a man to be a 'catch'.

A man may retain a roving eye into very old age provided he is in reasonably good health. I have seen

men flirt well beyond the age of
potency and they never lose the hope
of being aroused one last time.
In fact, men seem to view flirtation,
arousal and seduction as the
real staff of life.

Women, on the other hand, are more likely
to settle into an existence of appreciation
and shared interests, when libidinous
thoughts become rare.

There are, of course, exceptions to this.
I have come across female octogenarians
kept youthful by lovers half their age.

To conclude: flirtation is the civilizing
of a biological necessity.

PREDATOR OR PREY?

It is said that men are divided into two categories: gentlemen and cads.

The former never speak of their conquests, the latter boast about them ad infinitum.

A generation of sexual-equality crusaders have not altered one fundamental fact of nature:

men are sexual predators by way of their biological make-up, whereas women, no matter how liberated,

are sexual prey.
Before I incur the wrath of feminists,
let me qualify this: men like to behave
as if they are predators and
conquerors; women enjoy the conquest
for what it is – the ultimate
surrender of men.

Few men have not watched – and been terrorised by – the movie *Fatal Attraction*, which develops the theme of an obsessive female turning from prey into predator.

It led to the coining of the term 'bunny-boiler' for a violent, obsessive female stalker.

Both men and women can become victims or perpetrators of obsession with the opposite sex. Love has little or nothing to do with obsessional behaviour that is directed at another person.

Compulsive fixation is a symptom of a deeply rooted dissatisfaction with one's self: it often stems from a rigid upbringing that leads to loneliness and a lack of fulfilment.

Whatever its roots, it is both socially destructive and self-destructive. Psychologists do not view its related condition, jealousy, as a personality disorder but throughout history the 'green-eyed monster' has wreaked far more havoc on relationships between men and women.

Of course, strong emotions always override rational control, and some of us truly cannot control our jealousy or our possessiveness. Indeed, this lack of control – crime passionel – becomes almost seductive as it implies extreme devotion.

The majority of men present the following paradox: their egos receive a powerful boost when their partner is admired by other men.

Yet, they reflexively resent it being expressed and in some cases react violently. If they don't take the admirer to task, they may turn on the woman for having provoked the attention.

I have observed women who enjoy being the centre of attention.

They court it.

They walk ahead of their man and stare directly at whoever is walking towards them. This compels every man to stare back at them.

Their trailing partner is not aware that the attention is solicited not the result of spontaneous admiration.

Despite changing attitudes, epitomised and illustrated by such TV soaps as *Sex in the City*, it is still the man who usually initiates the 'chase' and assumes the role of 'predator'.

The most famous courtesans of all time have always known how to captivate their lovers rather than attempt to usurp man's traditional role.

A man can fall for the charms of a woman to the extent that he is unable to refuse her anything and will go to any lengths to be with her.

Men have betrayed their countries, committed acts of unfathomable recklessness, lost their own identity, a fortune or even an empire for the love of a woman.

Men read the *Kama Sutra* to brush up on their sexual technique. In fact, the book teaches the art of seduction — it seeks to instruct disciples in captivating their chosen partner or partners to such a degree that the object of the seduction literally falls under the seducer's or seductress's power.

It is like the seductress has cast a spell on the seduced to be obsessively in love with her...but only benignly. She is too wise to be wicked.

The power of seduction can be more potent than any drug. The woman who harnesses it and uses it to her advantage is referred to as a 'femme fatale' – a fatally attractive woman. And a woman who is capable of engendering that sense of fate and fatality in a man is capable of accomplishing almost anything.

SEX AND SENSUALITY

When a man has sated his thirst with water, he reaches for and enjoys a glass of wine far more than if he had drunk it when he was thirsty. And so it is with sex and sensuality.

For most, sex is a pleasurable biological necessity; for the sophisticated, sensuality is what tempts and gratifies their unfamished palate.

The sex-hungry man will gorge on a woman's body, he may say that he loves her, but really he will just have enjoyed the meal.

Eventually, though, his palate will tire of
the same meal and he will seek out other
dishes. After a time our senses become jaded
with any particular sensation – whether this
is a smell, a sound, a taste or a particular
form of sexual gratification. As always, there
are a number of popular and prescribed
ways of circumventing this fact.

The erotic is one. It is meant to whip
up the senses, so that new areas of sexual
pleasure are opened up. Many men find
explicit pictures and films intensely
stimulating. Others require a more tactile
approach, often painfully tactile.

There are whips and canes and all manner
of peculiar garments intended for this
purpose. Then some people are aroused by
what is dangerous, distasteful or grotesque,
and therefore 'forbidden' (whether by nature,
tradition or law).

Hence the advent of websites lurking in the shadows of the twilight Internet – child pornography, S&M, and other tawdry deviations. I am neither equipped for nor interested in summarising the pros and cons of such practices. That which debases is the domain of sexual freaks.

Then, there are the How-To guides.

I always marvel at people who buy erotic books to study the 'techniques' before trying them out on their lover.

In a similar vein sex therapists are available to instruct the inadequate or just plain ignorant.

Some of this, I am sure, has some merit, but it is to take the road to Blackpool and, personally, I much prefer Monte Carlo.

Seduction should be an act of sensuality, which the best lovers in the world instinctively grasp.

Sensuality is found in refining one's own and one's lover's sexual emotions

and sensibilities, this cannot come
from a book or an instructional course
on how to make love.

Rather, I should like to devote some
thoughts to how sensuality can help reinvent
a relationship or initiate an explosive one.

Touching a person like this or like that can
have an electrifying effect, but the only
way to establish how, where and with what
intensity that touch should be given is to
explore — and to take the time to explore.

Time has become a precious commodity and
few of us are capable of taking a breather.
Yet, forgetting the rest of the world and
learning to understand one's own sensuality
is absolutely imperative for perpetual and
accomplished seduction.

I list below some of the things that others
have told me they find sensual and seductive,
without making the pretence of providing
the reader with any sort of manual.
Titillation, perhaps...and cause for reflection.

DEFINITIONS OF
SENSUAL & SEDUCTIVE

'Naturally large or enhanced breasts,
blonde hair (even if the colour is enhanced),
provocative and suggestive dancing.'

This statement is an approximate,
condensed definition from a super-wealthy
Scandinavian ship owner, whose girlfriend
boasts all of the above attributes.

That she entices other men around a bar or
a dance floor, and flirts with waiters and
musicians alike, does not appear to detract

from her charms — in fact, it seems to be perceived as an added attraction.

Her lover positively basks in the attention she draws, even though his appreciation is at times tinged with dismay.

At the other end of the spectrum, I received the following statement on the subject of seduction, which I report verbatim — with the indulgence of the speaker:

'In its most conscious form it smacks of strategy and conquest, and that has never been my game, though it certainly is for almost everyone else, from peacocks to people.

'Let them have it, and be happy with it. What I am attracted to has nothing to do with seductiveness. This doesn't mean that beauty and allure, in whatever form, are inert to me. I'm typical enough to say better to have that as

well, than not, and I most certainly have
my particular subjective standards and
instinctual attractions…but ultimately
what matters is what's real and true, and
no amount of eye-batting, quite
figuratively speaking, is going to make it
otherwise, or will likely work with me.

'I'm well past the youthful – or just
superficial – point where surface
packaging is sufficient, or need to have a
display item on my arm. Of course, for
so many, the process of getting is often
far more fun and self-assuring in its
challenge, excitement, and success than
actually having. So for me, seduction
can be dispensed with. Just give me
laughs, intelligence, unlimited and
unrestricted mutual affection, a taste for
good music, walks to nowhere in
particular, good and unadorned sex and
lots of it, endless conversation from the
trivial to the profound to the absurd,

complete comprehension,
encouragement and support, empathy,
and total trust and fidelity. Then I'm a
happy guy.

'So, I suppose that in itself could be an
answer to the question… let alone that
it's probably no different or wishful
than anyone else's laundry list.'

Quite!

Most men I have interviewed, in fact, cite a
n intangible.

They say that seductive is what 'clicks' —
that undeniable chemistry that propels a
man towards a particular woman.

*A touch of mystery; concealing, rather
than revealing clothes; a way of*

undressing – slowly, rather than stripping; reciprocated longing and desire; the ability to 'yield' while retaining some initiative.

I recently had lunch with a young, charming, successful and very worldly man who, having elicited the title and subject matter of this book, pointed out some mannerisms (such as the way I held my glass of wine cupped between both hands) that signalled a seductive overture.

When I expressed a degree of bewilderment, he added that the true seductress lacked artifice: flirtation and seduction were natural to her.

However, my luncheon companion cited love and great friendship as the components of a lasting seduction.

Yet another man expressed similar sentiments – that a book entitled *How to be Seductive* is an impossible one to write, as 'seductiveness cannot be defined – you either have it or you don't'.

While I would agree to a point, I do believe that men and women alike can benefit from knowing – better and frankly – what makes them attractive to each other.

READING THE SIGNS

*Many a budding romance
(or great passion) has withered along
a twisted path strewn with
misunderstandings and
miscommunication.*

It is a wondrous moment when a man and a woman recognise the mutual attraction that will inevitably propel them into each other's arms. The act of flirtation prompted by such recognition is seductive in itself.

I have, in the course of my life, met many a

Lothario who believed in his foolproof
flirting technique.

Oddly, women almost always recognise it as
that – technique – and tend to fall for the
natural, slightly wacky and awkward approach.
For one thing, it signals the absence of
promiscuity.

I will describe the most elegant and discreet
act of flirtation I have ever come across.

I was sitting at a hotel bar, perusing
the dinner menu with my young son, when
I became aware that I was being observed by
a man sitting on the other side of the bar.

The attention was unobtrusive but
unmistakable. I acknowledged it equally
discreetly by way of looking in that general
direction and holding the man's eyes for
a split second.

That was all.

Moments later, he left without a glance
and certainly without addressing me –
we were, after all, total strangers.
Later still I asked for my bill. The attentive
stranger had already paid it, but had then
vanished so that I would not draw the
obvious conclusions.

I saw him again the following day – at
the exact same place – and the friends who
accompanied me on this occasion were so
impressed with my account of the previous
encounter that they sent him a drink and
initiated an introduction.

So what are the signs universally recognised
by men and women?

Some men perceive any attention – even
negative attention – as encouragement, or so

I am told by one who knows.

Girls learn from a very early age and without any instruction how to flirt. Coarse flirting begets coarse response, however, and few have mastered the art of flirting with finesse and at just the right level of discretion.

Too much discretion and a man feels frozen out; too little and he might consider the advances improper or interpret them as a sign of desperation.

The signs can be interpreted even when they are incredibly subtle.

Quite recently I put this to a test of sorts.

I was invited to a private party at a nightclub where most guests had never met before.

They had, nevertheless, arrived in small groups and tended to congregate as such.

Standing totally alone, I found myself the object of conversation between two men.

They looked in my direction as they talked. I moved towards a stairway, the end of which is a dead-end. There I stood for a few moments sipping wine.

Predictably, one of the two men made for the staircase even though it was obvious that he could not go past me.

I observed him walking across the room towards me and then, on a whim, I fixed my gaze upon the dancing crowds, ignoring him so completely that he walked past me.

He then had to make volte-face and walk down the stairs, looking incredibly embarrassed.

A sullen, smile-less look produces exactly the same result: men will recoil from the most attractive women in the room if they perceive rejection in store.

Learning to smile with one's eyes only is a great advantage in flirting with strangers.

A broad grin directed at a person you have never met before could either be embarrassing or too brazen an invitation.

The eyes, in fact, are the single most expressive part of a person. They can be used in flirting to express countless nuances.

The mouth is sensual, which is why women have learned to accentuate it by outlining and colouring with lipstick.

Study the movements of your lips in the mirror — we all have mannerisms and some are more or less attractive than others.

Smiling lights up any face, and with older women lifts the corners of what might otherwise be a droopy mouth. This is also true of older men. Men can be mesmerised by a woman's mouth and lips and the way she moves them — the associations are intensely erotic.

When we refer to 'body language', we mean the way the body is used to signal feelings or responses. In the context of flirting and seduction, it is vitally important.

For example, I once read that Jackie Kennedy had a habit of stroking her upper arm, a practice that men find especially sensual. Much is expressed by the body that moves in harmony and grace – or alluringly and suggestively.

It is quite possible to have both grace and allure.

Girls who go to finishing schools learn posture before anything else – how to sit, how to get up, how to get in and out of a car, how to progress across a room or a dance floor, and so on.

Models also learn how to walk so as to present their bodies to their best advantage.

Observe how they place one leg in front
of the other, tilting it slightly outwards
so that the knee appears slimmer and
better defined.
This exaggerates the movement of the hips,
hence the distinctive 'catwalk'.

Men use their attire and body movements
too, but to a much lesser extent.

Men and women communicate through
body signals before they meet. This is the
essence of flirting.

No matter how attractive the woman,
a man does not generally approach her
unless she gives some indication that
she is approachable and would welcome
the attention.

When I asked why this should be, I was reminded
that men have fragile egos and dread rejection.

Having engaged in a certain amount of eye contact, women almost subconsciously use their bodies to seduce from a distance.

Even the most demure sitting position, with legs crossed and a modest hemline, can be made to look incredibly alluring.

Study yourself in front of the mirror to see how the shape of your legs alters according to how they are positioned.

Never expose the unflattering side – we all have one.

Draw attention to the best part of your legs when you adopt flirting mode. Men will notice this.

A slim ankle above a pointed high-heeled feminine shoe is riveting...well to men, who notice everything sexy.

SEDUCING A WOMAN

I recently asked a male friend of mine if the familiar assertion that men think of sex every seven seconds is correct. He replied, 'No, men do not think of sex every seven seconds – they want to have it every second.'

While most men understand the difference between lust and love, few are capable of separating the two, especially in their youth.

It follows that the object of flirting – as far as men are concerned – is seduction, and the purpose of seduction is the gratification of lust.

Men, however, are not necessarily know-ledgeable about what makes a successful seducer; in addition, they are easily bruised by actual or perceived rejection.

If flirtation is a game, the object of that game is to bewitch the object of desire to a point where he or she is responsive in equal measure.

It is no accident that when men boast of their conquests, they inevitably cite their partners' ardour as supportive evidence.

The old chestnut about mutton dressed as lamb is mostly applied to women. But it is men who look the most pathetic when they

try to recapture their youth by dressing like
their sons or growing their hair long (it looks
fine in youth but ungroomed in middle age).

If you dress with flirting in mind, dress
comfortably and in what suits you best.

Most women can spot a man who is
unaccustomed to wearing a tie, and a
rented dinner jacket is a dead give-away.

Trying too hard betrays insecurity; but
not trying hard enough women find laddish
and crude.

Women are universally attracted to
fast talkers. The perennial
virtues – modesty, level-headedness,
honesty and the absence of
sins in general – do not excite a

woman's imagination. The quintessential 'bad boy' does, however.

Presence, personality and the ability to convey authority are a magnet.

Shy and self-effacing men may appeal to one's maternal instincts but they do not inspire great passion.

Women at the higher end of the social scale can be spellbound by the earthiness of a 'rough diamond'; and a scoundrel can exert endless fascination over a well-brought up woman.

History is full of women who fall for seemingly inadequate or unsuitable men.

The 'lady and the gamekeeper' match,
for example, is perpetrated continuously
through seduction and passion.

A man needn't understand women —
indeed, it is the mystery of how we are
different that makes us so alluring to
one another.

A man does, however, need to accept the
difference and use it to his advantage.

Whatever the circumstances, the act of
flirtation is opened with eye contact.

Women are highly literate in reading men's eyes
and are uncommonly accurate at interpreting
the significance of what they have read.

There is admiration, ogling, longing, lust…
and there is passing interest.

Women respond differently to the signals, depending on what they themselves expect of the moment. Mostly, they welcome the attention as it boosts their confidence and gives them reassurance.

Many men are intimidated and hesitant in the face of a very attractive woman.

This is because they erroneously believe that women who stand out for their natural beauty must either be taken or, if not, are extremely selective in respect of their countless other admirers.

But it is a mistake to think that attractive women do not require

reassurance. In fact, the need for

assurance increases in proportionate

to a woman's attractiveness.

Thus, many a beautiful girl is often left pining in secrecy. Men assume that she fights off offers constantly and, fearing rejection, he doesn't even try.

An exaggerated compliment always thaws the ice, and from then on it rather depends on how well the man is able to hold the woman's interest. Some men try to do this by attempting to impress her.

A man should never name-drop in front of a woman who is socially secure — she will find it ridiculous and dismiss him as a snob. There is an acceptable level of name-dropping, which is resorted to in order to establish 'social belonging' and common friends or background, but if there are any uncertainties it should be avoided.

Impressing a woman with the size of one's wallet or stock portfolio works...if it is done with subtlety.

However, many men make the mistake of listing their assets and business interests by way of introduction – as if they were submitting a business plan.

A buccaneering spirit, a sense of adventure and the intimation of an eventful background are more likely to hold a woman's interest than a dissertation on the futures and commodities exchange – unless perhaps she makes a living there herself.

Raw lust, though, is never a dampener.

It stirs in a woman a primeval instinct and she is drawn to its call, sometimes despite her cultural conditioning.

Passing interest is something a girl might engage in when she is cutting her teeth at the game of flirting.

On the other hand, unabashed ogling is offensive. Men ogle overtly either because they are not aware that they are doing it or in the mistaken belief that women are flattered by it.

Eye contact is more often than not followed by direct approach. Men's body language is quite precise, so a woman tends to know instinctively the moment when a man is about to address her.

While a confident man can initiate a
conversation with ease, what of those who
need some help?

Asking questions that necessitate a yes or
no answer stifles the conversation at the very
beginning, so these are best avoided.

It is often said that men who have a
sense of humour win hands down in the
seduction contest.

But beware: while women love to be
entertained, humour is a very subjective
thing. Crude jokes may be strangely
compelling to some women but can repel
a sensitive one.

A man's ability to listen to a woman
with genuine solicitude and a degree of
participation is greatly valued – listening is
an act of flattery.

I am inevitably drawn out of foul moods when asked questions about things that are much on my mind at that particular time. I am aware of the tactic but it works nonetheless.

Admiring other women – present or absent, dead or living, successful, clever, or famous – is hurtful and does nothing to enhance a man's chances of success in seduction.

Many years ago, a man committed the faux pas of telling me of his admiration for Brigitte Bardot. In my mind, I dispatched him to try to chat her up.

Reminiscences of past romance are equally dampening, unless unfavourably compared to the present relationship – whether existing or budding.

Men who are adept at flirting know that a woman enjoys the illusion of being pursued – even if she has initiated the contact herself.

The man should be possessive but not excessively jealous. Most women prefer a man who 'marks his territory'; if he doesn't, the implication is that he doesn't care enough.

Old-fashioned good manners and chivalry have been denounced as things of the past over and over again, but only a few misguided women find them superfluous or unwelcome.

The man should aim to be protective. Even the most independent woman loves the idea of having a supportive arm around her shoulders.

Romance is man's best friend in the flirtation game.

Women love receiving flowers, cards, scent, and dinner, theatre or concert invitations. They also love a man who can dance — not just the solitary, modern version of dancing, but the kind that allows a man the opportunity to register his interest both publicly and innocently, and to hold her close and whisper sweet nothings in her ear.

When women dance rhythmically, they do so either for themselves or to impress or seduce a man.

In contrast, a man gyrating by himself on a dance floor is a lame image of virility indeed.

Men of a certain age find flirting a chore as

it requires an effort. But as with all hard work it also pays dividends, and one forgets at times just how much fun flirting can be.

WHAT MAKES A SEDUCER?

This is all very well, you might say, but what leads to a seduction?

More often than not it is a matter of chemistry, although even if there is no chemistry a woman might persuade herself that it is there provided she is offered the right cocktail of wealth and power.

Power, as Henry Kissinger once observed, is the ultimate aphrodisiac. It is no accident that politicians are rarely monogamous.

How a man works the chemistry when it is present is left to his instincts, experience and confidence.

Seduction is a matter of touch – at the right time, with the right intensity and in the right place.

A brush across the face can trigger more longing in a woman than mauling. Women always fall for the romantic gesture. A single flower picked from a field can melt the coldest reserve.

Of course, a man's greatest weapon is – as it has ever been – flattery.

Women are vain, so a feel for the compliment is crucial.

Assuming that a woman should feel flattered

because she is the focus of one's attention could lead to misinterpretation.

Women need to be told what is attractive about them in the physical sense — and they need to be told this frequently.

If you are unsure, take a thesaurus and look up all the words synonymous with the one word that best describes your lover's (or prospective lover's) most attractive feature.

Then use these words liberally. When used to conjure up the right imagery, words are a potent turn-on for women. Thus, many a modern relationship has been born over the Internet through electronically 'spoken' words.
In fact, some relationships are sustained with just words... Flirtation usually begins with a certain look, but words carry it through to the next stage — seduction.

Along with talk, women are susceptible to touch. Once the ice has been broken, the object of a man's desire can be his if with lust in his eyes he simply starts to become more tactile.

Of course, any woman of a certain intellect will see through this and will look for a more challenging conversation, yet she may still succumb to the technique.

Physical seduction, which is what the majority of men are intent on, is usually mediated by a successful flirtation that has developed and deepened over time, but it can also be the end product of a momentary fancy.

Neither feminism nor political correctness have altered our nature.

Volumes have been devoted to the subject of libido and what makes a successful lover.

Men will never know and women will never tell when desire and pleasure are exactly matched in two people.

It is often said that women 'fake' ardour in lovemaking. However, if a man has taken the trouble to awaken the senses of a woman, he will know that there is no faking.

Sustaining the curve of desire is the secret of a great seducer. That curve of desire in a man is vertiginous, whereas in a woman it is tortuous and hardly ever straightforward. When the two run in tandem and meet there is a spark. A man who knows how to achieve this can seduce not just a woman's body but her soul too.

Women love being seduced; but they also love playing seductress.

So there often comes a time when seduction stops being a game orchestrated by the man, and the seducer is himself seduced — which leads us on to the next chapter.

SEDUCING A MAN

I have bad news. What women always suspected of men is true: men are visually attracted to the opposite sex.

Having elicited numerous frank comments on the subject, I can confirm that if the brightest, sweetest, kindest, wittiest girl is also nondescript or dowdy in appearance she does not stand a chance next to the dullest harpy endowed with a pair of long shapely legs.

Typically, a man first notices whichever part of a woman's anatomy drives his fantasies. With some it is legs, others breasts, for many it is posterieurs, but once a slim ankle in a woman was enough to inflame the male's imagination.

Pondering this, I wondered what endeared Hillary Clinton to her philandering husband, the ex-president of the United States, since the New York senator is hardly blessed with long slim legs or, for that matter, delicate ankles.

I put this to the sort of men who should know. Their responses ranged from bawdy jokes to sartorial advice on the wearing of trouser suits.

It takes all kinds to make the world, my grandmother used to say, and it is as well that men's tastes differ.

After all, if they did not they would all be lusting after the same few beauties and the human population would shrink dramatically.

> *But after the bad news comes the good – there is something in all of us that will appeal to one particular man who will find us irresistibly attractive.*

Provocative clothing is one factor that can be used to attract men's attention, but there are a lot of myths that surround this idea, and so I shall take this opportunity to dispel some of them.

DRESSING SEDUCTIVELY

When a woman is very young she needs little or no enhancement.

Yet girls often assume that revealing a great deal of flesh makes them more interesting to men.

While no red-blooded male would ever bemoan the return of the mini skirt or hot pants, or complain about low-cut, transparent tops, most men instinctively respond to the erotic appeal of a glimpse of flesh as opposed to seeing it all.

Bearing this in mind, I want to explore how to dress seductively. After all, the male's first impression of a woman counts for far more than vice versa.

Rule one is to dress appropriately – for one's age, for the occasion and for the season. Dressing mutton up as lamb is a common mistake.

Conversely, young women often apply too

much make-up in the attempt to look more mature.

Tight-fitting garments do nothing for the figure. In a slim woman they suggest cheap tailoring or hint at vulgarity, while in heavier women they emphasise the surplus weight.

Loose garments make the figure look more svelte than it is, but note that baggy garments look sloppy and frumpy.

Some women are more suited to the 'gamine' look. They are petite and slender, with not a hint of voluptuousness. This type of woman looks best in slightly masculine clothing, which adds great allure and sensuality to her.

But, by and large, men prefer women to dress in a way that highlights their femininity.

Different social occasions dictate different

dress codes. Someone once described to me how a wealthy American with great social aspirations attempted to make her sartorial mark at a race meeting.

She donned a sequinned denim jacket and snakeskin boots, no doubt in a bid to outshine the frumpy British horsewomen who adopt a practical look and would not trade their Wellington boots and jumpers for all the tea in China.

Such overdressing smacks of insecurity and trying too hard. Under-dressing shows disregard for your host or hostess and for the occasion.

Rule two is dress appropriately for the venue or event.

Learning what the balance is comes with age and experience, but it can be mastered by all.

Dressing in a designer label for the label itself shows lack of imagination unless it is done with thought for one's figure, personality and individual style. We all have our favourite labels.

For some of us, our choice is dictated by budget; for others, individual taste can be expressed without consideration for cost.

In either case, adopting an individual style is the key to establishing a personal image.

Rule three *then is do
not let the label, or garment,
'wear' you and overwhelm
your personality.*

Rule four is dress for the season.

When I was a young girl I fought endless
battles with my mother over my wish to
wear my favourite blouse – a sleeveless
silk top – come rain or shine.

Wearing such a garment in the middle
of winter makes the wrong statement: it
shows desperation to impress and a lack of
judgement (aside from which it is difficult
to look seductive when one is freezing cold).

If you dress in a way that does not fit the
weather or season, as well as looking out of

sorts you would feel uncomfortable.

It is vital to feel comfortable in one's clothes. Feeling at ease projects a more confident image and allows you to focus on flirtation – not on the tightness of your belt or the fact that your hem is riding up your thighs when you don't want it to.

Rule Five*: Above all, wear clothes that flatter your figure, not the garment that looks best on Claudia Schiffer, Kate Moss or whoever your role model may be. Be your own role model and learn to like yourself. This will give you the confidence that sets attractive women apart.*

While many women know what clothing is seductive, that they don't always choose to wear such garments (or undergarments) has to do with habit, comfort and state of mind.

We all know that men love silky sensual lingerie and stockings rather than tights.

Yet certain women only wear stockings on special occasions when they are looking to please a man.

Now stockings are far more hygienic than tights but my point is this:

> *Wearing sensual underwear without*
> *the expectation of it being seen*
> *by anyone other than you makes*
> *you feel sensual, and it shows.*

It puts you in a certain state of mind —
just as wearing an old dressing gown
and greying cotton knickers puts you in
an opposite one.

In terms of appearance, you are what you
wear at any one moment. Learn to dress in
such a way that you feel attractive to
yourself. Wearing transparent clothes, or
showing bare flesh or underwear is tacky
and men react to this accordingly.

The 'come hither' look may produce instant
results, but men who respond primarily to
female flesh are emotionally barren.

The streetwalker look is for those who
charge for sex not the seductress in search
of romance.

Do not cheat — or at least not blatantly —
in your dress.

Excessive bra padding is misleading and could cause severe disappointment if it has been turned into a selling point. Imagine the scene when the object of your seduction techniques is faced with reality...

Instead, enhance your best features. High heels, for example, exist for a specific reason: they serve the purpose of lifting a woman's posterieur into a provocative position as well as making the legs look longer and better toned.

But they lose all raison d'être if they are worn, as unfortunately is so often the case, with baggy trousers or a loose, full-length dress or coat.

The dress rule that makes an exception of every other rule is that simplicity is always best.

Elegance stems from simplicity, and elegance is alluring and seductive in a very special way – it puts a woman on a whole different level.

MAKE UP

Make-up is highly individual.

A friend of mine calls it 'war paint', which is precisely what it is: an artifice and another arrow in the quiver for seduction warfare.

Do not follow the trends created by the cosmetic companies' eternal recycling of product. This is to be a make-up victim. Do not let yourself be exploited by the marketing ploys of the cosmetic giants.

Essentially, we are born with a certain complexion and bone structure.

Whether you are targeted to buy gold eye shadow or flesh-coloured lipstick this season and smoky-grey eye shadow and scarlet lip gloss the next, your face remains the same, and that is all you have to take into consideration.

Brunettes look washed out in pale beige colours; blondes look garish in strong colours.

Too much eye colour precludes the use of a strong lip colour – it creates an over painted look. Eye pencil may make the eyes look larger but it also ages them.

Most women need some colour on their cheeks if they do not have it naturally. The most – and perhaps only – seductive make-up is lipstick.

Outlining the lips with pencil makes them look fuller (without a hint of the 'trout pout' look). Red lipstick – in all its permutations and shades – has a direct sexual symbolism that always inflames the male's fantasies.

ENHANCEMENTS DO THEY WORK?

Most men scoff at the idea of surgical or other artificial enhancements.

So why are plastic surgeons, hair colourists and sundry enhancement specialists so popular and sought after?

Because most men – while disdainful of the vanity it represents and resentful of the expense – appreciate the benefits of the improvement.

Even semi-permanent interventions – such as hair colouring, botox and collagen injections, and so on – can have a dramatic effect on a woman's appearance with the advantage that they do not require a healing period.

The popularity of breast-enhancement surgery remains undiminished despite the risks it presents to the long-term health of women.

Watching an erotic dancing show in a club recently, I enquired of the men I was sitting with if they found the dancers desirable. The younger of my companions pointed to one of the girls and remarked that she would be perfect if her breasts hadn't been so exaggeratedly pumped up with silicone.

The comment was a surprising one as I had harboured the belief that men couldn't tell the difference – between nature and silicone, that is.

I have met women who are able to (and do) spend a fortune on stalling the ravages of time. They look perpetually in their thirties – even when they are two decades older.

What does it matter if others are aware of the subterfuge? These women are almost universally admired and envied.

Enhancement – when it is carried out professionally (and you must try to get the best in the field) and done in moderation (surgical excesses are well documented and highly humiliating) – can do wonders for one's self-esteem as well as for the physical image one presents to the world.

Talking about it, however, is anything but seductive.. If you decide to have some sort of enhancement, let it remain your secret.

WHAT MAKES A SEDUCTRESS?

Once flirtation has produced the desired result, what is the most compelling factor (beyond a deep cleavage) that holds the man's attention?

What is it that separates a great seductress from just another pretty face?

For an attractive face and a desirable body alone are not sufficient by a long shot.

Men, it has been confirmed time and again, love talking about themselves when trying

to make an impression. A woman
who knows how to listen is halfway
there. Listening alone is not enough,
however. Hearing what is being said,
showing interest, admiration,
fascination – all are important.

Make a man feel as if he is the only one left
on the planet and he will find you fascinating.

Be a mirror that tells him that he is the
greatest in this world (or in yours, at the
very least).

Be sparkly, effervescent, audacious and
funny; never discuss any of your ailments
and physical indispositions with him.
Men are justly wary of anything that smacks
of "Not tonight dear, I have a headache".

Besides, they do not really want to know if your desirable body has hidden warts or gives you trouble.

Your body is a pleasure machine – one that gives pleasure and one that a man likes to give pleasure to.

Show him how to do that but do not be explicit or forward about it.

Many men's sensibilities are offended if a woman indulges in men's locker-room chat. Being sensual is fine and interest in the erotic is great, but instructions on the mechanics of sex suggests that your partner is somehow remiss or even inadequate.

Allow yourself some fragility – vulnerability even.

Men are programmed to feel protective and are often confused by the dictates of political correctness, which would have women equal in every respect.

Determination, strength of character and knowing what you want are fine and admirable.

But do impress on a man that he is needed. We all like to feel needed.

A certain vulnerability in men can be endearing if it does not border on weakness, whereas vulnerability and fragility in a woman – both physical and emotional – can be her strength.

I once enquired of a mixed panel of email correspondents whether youth is seductive.

Curiously, the women seemed to **believe** this more so than **the men.**

Chivalry aside, men do appreciate sensuality, whatever the age of the woman.

The greatest seductress of all time, as far as I am concerned, was Wallis Simpson, Duchess of Windsor.

I once asked the late Duchess of Argyll what she thought of her. She described her as anodyne.

I could not dismiss this as envy, for Margaret Argyll was a much-admired beauty in her day and until she died had the confidence to be generous to other women.

I knew that Margaret's description was not uncharitable but I still felt it was wrong.

Wallis Simpson was neither very young when she met the Prince of Wales nor a conventional beauty by a long stretch of the imagination.

Yet, she already had two marriages under her belt and so beguiled her prince that he renounced the throne rather than let her go.

Whispers abound about her prolonged stay in the Far East and the erotic secrets she might have learned there.

I suspect the truth to be rather more complex. Wallis Simpson possessed a highly individual style and unerring taste.

She looked delicate to the point of frailness and appealed to men's need to protect. She was, by all accounts, witty (read her letters to her aunt), charming and attentive.

She must have made the prince feel special and unique – no small accomplishment, considering he was a man already surrounded by countless sycophantic courtiers.

It may be that she was also more inventive in bed than the prince's mistress at the time, but this is pure conjecture.

A contemporary example is the current Prince of Wales' long-term companion, Camilla Parker-Bowles.

She possesses neither the youth nor the willowy figure of the late Princess Diana, yet the Prince clearly preferred her to his wife. What do such women have in common?

Ask a man and he is likely to be non-plussed. He can hardly point to parts of their anatomy or cite their youth.

He might mention common interests,
intelligence, sense of humour...

The answer I am sure is that Wallis Simpson
and Camilla Parker-Bowles practised what all
great seductresses know:

*Every man appreciates a woman
who shows she exclusively admires
him and him alone.*

WHERE AND
WHEN TO FLIRT

Social flirting is mostly played out in a
controlled environment — at a party, for
example, where one is expected to circulate
and engage in flirtation.

There is an acceptable level of flirting at parties.
An old roué once described social flirtation
in these terms: 'I flirt with every female
I meet — pour la politesse.'

What he meant was that it would be
impolite not to — a woman would feel
singularly unattractive if she did not get
chatted up at a party.

The man who uttered the above gem added that this kind of polite flirtation 'led nowhere' – in other words, it did not lead to a romp in bed.

But, as we know, flirting can have another purpose. It could be used to displace a rival, succeed at an interview or an audition, obtain a discount, get someone to help you or to do you a small favour, generate sympathy, engender good will, minimise some damage and so on.

Flirting is a form of flattery, which is why it is so winsome and versatile. Those subjected to it feel wanted, desired, valued...

THE PLACE

There are, in various parts of the world, establishments where the atmosphere is singularly conducive to flirting.

The ability to create such an atmosphere, without any tackiness (a 'pick-up joint' is tacky), is an art in itself, and those club/bar owners who have succeeded enjoy faithful cosmopolitan clientele.

Regular visitors to Monte Carlo (as well as those based there all the year round) would unanimously point to the Sass Café as a perfect example of the above.

Describing its atmosphere is impossible; suffice it to say that the place, with its boudoir-like decor, eclectic live music and relaxed opening hours, the suave presence of the owner and the clever mixture of restaurant/piano bar/dancing space (the latter is very limited, but does not appear to deter the patrons) is an absolute haven for rather sophisticated revellers who find themselves in need of company, or who just need to alleviate the feeling of solitude.

While Sass is not the only such establishment, it wins hands down in my list of preferences at the moment.

Generally speaking, establishments that have a drinking area or offer bar meals are conducive to starting a conversation.

Green's of St James's in London has some space at the bar where one can order a plate of oysters and admire the sporting pictures. Service is unobtrusive and patrons are well able to strike up conversation. Another good place is Motcomb's. Walk into the bar (there is also a restaurant and a night-club) on any one evening, sit by the bar and, chances are, you will end up spending the rest of that evening in some congenial company.

I have noticed that many patrons travel some distance to go there for a drink, which gives the place the je ne sais quoi that distinguishes it from the many other establishments that attempt to emulate it.

Some of the new London clubs appear to have precisely the mixture – sophisticated and interesting patrons, a good DJ, and a club feeling (for most of them are members-only) – that makes flirtation not only possible but worth engaging in.

Noble Rot and Attica are among those that merit a mention here.

Hotel bars are not always as good a place as you might imagine – unless, of course, you are a resident.

Even the venerable American Bar at the Hôtel de Paris seems to have suffered a small, albeit discreet invasion of attractive blonde girls (most sound Russian), who size up every unaccompanied man walking in.

The American Bar, I hasten to add, is not a place for flirtation. The tables are too well spaced out to abet casual intimacy. More-over, a sophisticated staff and maître d' are picky about their clientele.

You get a table there only if you fit the bill – looking down at heel or too call-girlish meets with a polite but still a very chilly cold shoulder.

The Bull and Bear bar at the Waldorf Astoria in New York is where stockbrokers meet at the end of a day. There they relax with a glass of champagne — or beer — and chat up some of the single ladies who go with similar ideas in mind.

There are countless other more or less formal establishments where one can strike up an easy conversation with a stranger. The bar at the Mayflower Hotel in Washington DC is flirtation-friendly, while its Willard and Hay Adams counterparts are more forbidding.

Both the lobby and the bar at Badrutt's Palace in St Moritz are in a league of their own. To begin with the hotel is frequented by dateable 'beautiful people'. The spirit of a shared sporting interest makes it easier for them to establish off-piste connections — and they often do.

The Cipriani Hotel in Venice stands in its own grounds, and guests are encouraged to indulge in the fantasy of being a part of a private house party.

Formality notwithstanding (for this is a grand and formal hotel), engaging in conversation with a fellow hotel guest is easy while lunching in the garden or sitting by the pool. One is secure in the knowledge that the person thus spoken to 'belongs'.

This is also true of the Villa d'Este Hotel on Lake Como.

Paris has a myriad outdoor terraces that are open all year round, as do Cannes and St Tropez.

Few of them are conducive to flirting, however – most are frequented by tourists who stop for a drink, either because they are exhausted or because they have heard that Fouquets is the place to sit and watch the world go by.

The terrace of the Carlton Hotel in Cannes may be the exception that comes to mind. One can lunch there (the terrace is an extension of the very elegant indoor restaurant) or just have a drink and observe the endless flow of patrons. As the terrace is not at street level but somewhat raised, the casual passer-by is deterred. One frequents the Carlton Terrace Bar with intent...

Avoid the dining hours in drinking-only establishments. It is best to go before or after dinner — whatever time it is customary to take that meal in a particular country. In the United States, this might be as early as six o'clock. In the Mediterranean, it might be as late as ten or even eleven o'clock, although the traditional time is nine.

*The smaller and more formal the place,
the harder it is to attract the
attention of your target.
Conversely, the larger and rowdier it is
the more you are likely to feel
the object of a 'pick up' rather than
the strategist of a 'seduction
campaign'.*

In conclusion, flirting with a stranger in a public place is a minefield.

Yet, as with all somewhat perilous pursuits, it is highly enjoyable and gives many an incomparable rush of adrenalin.

Beware of addicts!

THE ETIQUETTE OF FLIRTING

When I spoke of this book to a friend, describing it as an exploration of the flirting and mating game, he rightly observed with a smile that the aim as in any game is to 'score'.

It is certainly true that today's relaxed morality and increased appetite for self-gratification at any cost makes it easy to confuse seduction with, well, scoring.

However, scoring is for the famished and the immature. Seduction is for grown-ups and for connoisseurs – those who take the time to appreciate both the thrill of anticipation and the joy of getting there.

When I was growing up, the cardinal rule was that a woman never spoke to a man unless she was first introduced by a third party.

This has now changed dramatically and the etiquette of modern flirting does not preclude a woman from taking the initiative.

But more traditional men may still find this slightly off-putting and, sexual liberation notwithstanding, it is still the male who generally initiates the first contact.

It is extremely difficult for a woman to do this elegantly and without giving the wrong impression.

The theatre, the opera or a concert hall, as well as a children's playground, are a few of the venues where a woman can approach a man without inviting derogatory remarks.

In such places a polite enquiry as to whether the man is enjoying the performance, or a child-orientated comment, is acceptable.

The racecourse is another 'safe' ground, where a woman can address a strange man with comments on a horse, a jockey, a car or anything else related to racing without some derogatory inference being drawn.

Many people strike up a conversation on the dance floor, as it is now quite customary for men and women to dance individually. The success of such an approach depends almost entirely on the state of inebriation of both parties.

Engaging a total stranger in the act of seduction requires confidence and a certain awareness of flirting etiquette.

If your attention is caught by a man sitting at what appears to be an unbridgeable distance from you, you indicate interest by what comes automatically to us all: with the eyes and with subtle body language.

A relentless stare would embarrass the more demure and is in any case bad manners. The eyes can express a hint of a smile without the mouth following suit.

Lifting a glass to one's lips can represent a sign of complicity – especially when acknowledged and reciprocated.

A repeated glance in someone's direction is perfectly well understood by both sexes.

Whether, or how, it is carried further depends on circumstances, one's sense of propriety (to approach a person who is accompanied is tacky) and not least on one's ingenuity and confidence as a person.

If a woman is clearly not accompanied by a husband or a 'date' and is simply in a group of friends, it is acceptable to send a drink to them all. It is not acceptable to send a drink to her only.

Asking a waiter to present your card is another option.

If you send a drink to a single woman, do not press your advantage.

While the gracious thing for her to do is to accept it, she should not be made to feel that acceptance equals an obligation to invite you to join her at her table.

Nor should you beckon her to join you. If she responds, she is not worth seducing; if she does not, you will, in fact, have spoiled your chances of moving the encounter along.

If you are a woman, and you have accepted a drink from a stranger, you should lift your glass in acknowledgement and leave it at that.

The man will then be left to judge whether or not to make the next move; and this will depend on the invitation in your smile – or the absence of it.

It is the woman's prerogative to say no and she should never relinquish that.

If you want to be sure that he does make the next move, then recruit intermediaries or even a waiter to ensure that he receives your card and telephone number...

There are men who find it exceedingly difficult to approach a woman in a bar or a restaurant. Such men would strike a conversation on the ski slopes or at the tennis court but lack the confidence to walk those few steps to a stranger's table.

An open smile would provide them with some encouragement, but really you need to offer them a conversation opener.

I am partial to the odd cigarillo. Recently a man sitting at the neighbouring table in a restaurant offered to swap one of his cigars with mine.

He expressed astonishment and delight at the fact that a woman appreciated cigars.

While women are seen smoking cigars fairly regularly these days, my interlocutor saw this as a conversational opportunity.

A book, a newspaper article, a fetching hat, a dog or an unusual adornment all provide such openings – but they must be 'given life', an indication that you would not mind being engaged in conversation on a particular topic.

A man who takes his flirting seriously – i.e., he flirts in pursuit of a sexual encounter – defines the etiquette of it thus:

'Flirtation should be so subtle that it leaves the object of one's attentions slightly unsure as to what is at stake.
        'The key is reciprocity. Play as if you both have equal hands, so never overbid and only raise the ante with her complicity.

'Physical contact — not of an overtly sexual nature — and the response to it give a fair indication of how far one can press one's attentions. If the interest is not there, each can exit the play with their egos intact.'

There are, of course, many who see no need for etiquette and dispense with it as they do with anything that requires an effort. The trouble with shortcuts is precisely that they do not allow for savouring the detail. But observing some form of etiquette separates the sophisticate from the oaf.

Finally, never forget the cardinal rule: flirting is for the unattached. Whether you are accompanied by your partner or you are on your own, you cut a pathetic rather than a dashing figure if you engage in real seductive chat-up.

Women reserve their most scathing epithets for such Lotharios, while men make their coarsest comments on the subject of philander-ing females.

Remember, etiquette is ultimately all about good taste.

WHEN THE
CHASE IS OVER

While many revel in the act of the one-off, casual chase and success, many others wish to perpetuate the seduction, either for a time or – if love exists and is reciprocated – forever more.

CAN A SEDUCTION
LAST FOREVER?

Opinions certainly differ:

Along with the results of various studies on the subject, there are our own romantic beliefs and expectations, there are also our

cultural ideals about love and fidelity —
especially as these are defined in the context
of marriage.

One recent study asserts that lust can last
only for some two to three years at most,
after which any enduring relationship has
to be based on a multitude of other bonds,
none of which has anything to do with
seduction or physical desire.

This is a pretty unromantic state of affairs,
but many a randy man would attest to the
truth of it.

Indeed, the Marquess of Bath has carried
this to its logical conclusion and, for all of
his adult life, has openly practised polygyny.

He has collected over seventy wifelets.
Whether that includes a similar duplication
of mother-in-laws we are not told.

Obviously the relationship between young lovers in the first throes of unbridled passion is different from the same couple embarking on married life nor will it be the same if they stay together into middle age.

Passion does burn itself out and cannot alone sustain a relationship over a lifetime.

Some middle-aged couples accept the reality of passion spent but accommodate to it by leading double lives.

I do know of one such relationship, which is kept afloat with much artifice as well as by the thrill of indiscretion — both risk much from public exposure.

They also have to contend with lengthy absences from each other, but at the end of each such absence gratification is doubled in intensity.

The artifice is provided by elaborate 'toys', which both lovers delight in finding and putting to use.

However, such continuous 'lashing' of the senses involves a quasi-obsession with sex and erotica. Such a solution to the problem produces a more malignant condition.

There is a certain wisdom in accepting that living with some problems is better than trying to solve them. Life is for living not perfecting.

When the chase is over, most of us want — or even need — commitment.

Studies tell us that single people (and this is especially true of men) are less healthy and happy and live fewer years.

As a rule, single people yearn for a relationship. This is continuously reaffirmed by the proliferation of personal ads both in newspapers and on the Internet.

A passing survey into what motivates male advertisers attests to the fact that, rather than perceiving their single status as the gate to sexual liberty and adventure, they are alarmed by it and view it as a sign of inadequacy.

So they are willing to suffer the indignity of unseemly self-promotion to alleviate their loneliness. The descriptions in Lonely Heart columns make most of us cringe but clearly they serve their purpose.

Men advertise more than women but many more of the latter are genuine. For many of the men, this is just another 'pulling ground' for sex; whereas women tend to want what they say they do – a relationship.

Actually these women are by no means all middle-aged or beleaguered lone parents.

Ads abound describing gorgeous blondes yearning for stability and companionship (for that is what most female advertisers seem to cherish above all).

During my research for this book, I became intrigued with one fundamental contradiction in the wording of these ads – generally the advertisers describe themselves in glowing terms, which are utterly at odds with the inadequacy that is intrinsic to what they are doing.

To tease this out I conducted my own straw poll and asked a sample of advertisers the same question:

Why is it that the success they speak of has not translated into meeting

someone in the course of their
social lives?

Everyone I spoke to claimed not to be able to engage in romance in the context of their business and social relationships. They further claimed in as many words that they were seeking that special 'chemistry'.

Yet the latter is elusive enough in even propitious circumstances, let alone in the context of having to select likely candidates from the replies, then interview them!

I suspect that some advertisers
become addicted to the sense of
novelty this form of interaction offers.
It is a means to spice up their
otherwise dull lives. Yet, the 'magic'

*they seek will always be one step
ahead, eternally eluding them as they
chase after it.*

POST-SEDUCTION STAGES

Much has been written about how we in the
West, despite rising prosperity, better health
and increased protection from the ills of the
rest of the world, lead unfulfilled lives.

Too much is expected of us...not least in the
area that is the subject of this book.

*Of men, society demands seductive
and sexual prowess, financial success,
ability to negotiate the maze of
modern and often contradictory*

mores, social awareness
and responsibility and so on.

When all this begins to look and feel like a yoke, many call a 'timeout'. Thus, mid-life is when men have the most affairs, and not just one-night stands.

Such liaisons are erotically charged and, at this stage, potentially life-changing.

For women, modern society has contrived to create a set of impossible ideals that must nevertheless be achieved if a woman is not to feel a failure.

Today's woman is expected to have her own glittering career while at the same time continuing to be a support to her success-ful husband's; she must have perfect children to whom she is an intelligent and caring mother, while at the same time preserving her youthful pre-childbirth looks!

For both spouses children are a major test, as are travel, jobs, promotions, mortgages, nannies...

Modern life is also rife with temptations.

The office affair is quite common, but so are affairs between married friends.

Simply being presented with the opportunity to seduce (or be seduced) is a test in itself.

With all this for couples to contend with, surviving mid-life crisis and keeping a relationship relatively intact should be considered nothing less than a triumph.

When the mystery is gone from a relationship and there is nothing left to explore or conquer, seduction becomes a mechanical ritual.

If familiarity breeds contempt, repetitiveness breeds boredom: it is commonplace for men who are bored to play the field while women who are bored bolt.

After the arrival of children many men begin to look elsewhere for excitement, and women are inevitably hurt by this.

That is not to say that women do not indulge in pursuing excitement, but they tend to do this later in life when their children are more self-sufficient.

(Autumnal women can be very passionate

indeed, knowing as they do that their attractiveness is in its last bloom.)

I once asked an ageing philanderer what
compelled him to stray even though he
had a beautiful wife some twenty years his
junior. His reply was metaphorically revealing:
'I like caviar very much, but I wouldn't want
to live on a perpetual diet of it alone.'

He was rich enough to afford as much
caviar and young women as he wanted,
but in buying sex (naturally he did not
see his 'presents' as payment) he was
precluded from the delights of seduction
and romance.

*It is recognised that young men, for all
their romanticism, favour playing the
field – they see status in quantity*

rather than in quality. Seldom does a youthful seduction result in a long-lasting match.

Expecting a young lover to remain interested, let alone faithful, is hopeless, although older women, skilful in the art of pleasing and using their bodies, are sometimes able to perpetuate the seduction for a long while.

Thus, young men can become besotted with a seductress who does not nag, play games, cry for attention, or worry about feathering a nest or procreating, but who at the same time dispenses her passion freely.

Women often lapse into a state of complacency, especially after the euphoria of producing a first child.

*A man's gratitude for
his progeny does not last
long, and it certainly does
not obliterate his own need to
be shown attention
– and given priority.*

Women with successful marriages have always put their husbands before their children.

This is not to say that they are negligent or unloving mothers, but rather that they establish a particular order that children understand and respect: parents are a unit that has its own secret dynamics.

The unit functions irrespective of the children, who may often be excluded from it. But they need not feel any less loved for that.

This was so in the family in which I grew up, where the adults were self-involved and mutually preoccupied.

Tempers were explosive at times and passions unleashed frequently. Various little dramas were forever smouldering, but we children were uninvolved.

Without witnessing such happenings, we were nonetheless aware of discords and reconciliations. In short, our parents and grandparents had live relationships and took each other seriously; while they let us live out our childhood and adolescence.

Women go through stages when they find a substitute for physical desire and gratification. Men do not sublimate so – they stray.

Women should understand this...
which is not the
same as accepting it

In the child-rearing stage, women frequently write their own book of doom by focusing disproportionately on the home: state-of-the-art kitchens, special bathrooms and interior-designed reception rooms become a semi-obsession and the main object of pride and desire.

Excessive tidiness, time spent dreaming about colour schemes, social cachet as embodied by one's address and choice of friends, competitiveness...these can all send a man crazy and drive him away. Such a man might go from enjoying his home as his 'lair' to craving the carefree, clutter-happy days of his bachelorhood.

I know one such man who, having divorced an ambitious and aggressive woman, has happily disposed of all the props of financial success and lives in a throwback to his student digs.

He would not marry again unless he fell hopelessly in love but, even then, the survival mechanism might prevent him from walking into what he would see as 'another trap'.

Women also agonise over their own and their husbands' careers in a way that is different from men. For most men, a career is an economic imperative.

For women, the material indicators of success – as measured by the yardstick of their peers' standard of living – are the basis of their self-esteem.

Being married to a man who cannot provide such status symbols is keenly felt by many women as a stigma attached directly to them.

Communicating such a feeling to a man – especially one who is artistically engaged or still busy making a mark — is always demoralising.

Yet, for a variety of reasons, most men try to satisfy their wives' expectations: because they are genuinely in love; for the sake of peace; because they dislike change; for their children's sake.

But passion suffers as a result of these marital conflicts and compromises.

A woman, though, who rejects her husband too often risks driving him into the arms of another. Submitting to sex may not be much better but when desire is absent, on balance it is better to resort to artifice than to show a blatant lack of interest.

Even if desire is present, monotony and a lack of imagination can cause men to indulge in fantasies fuelled by countless publications created for this purpose.

KEEPING PASSION GOING

An old French saying professes that, 'Where there is embarrassment there is no pleasure.' To put aside one's inhibitions and to abandon oneself to passion is intoxicating.

Abandonment in all its facets means indulging and prompting one's imagination and that of one's partner.

It is no coincidence that the most frequently cited reason men give for going with a prostitute is to obtain something that they cannot ask for, or be offered, at home. For all that, stimulation has to be spiritual as well as sexual.

At the outset of each day a woman should try to revive the same awe and excitement that first lit the passion. Of all the things she has chosen, this is the one that she should do with all her heart.

Only she can.

The seductress is always truer than the seducer.

The fulcrum between the excitement of this and the sense of security that a man derives from being the object of constant love and tenderness is where real happiness lies. Elusive yes, but oh so potent.

KEEPING ROMANCE ALIVE

Again and again we face the paradox that

lighting the fire is different from keeping it burning.

Then there is the issue of how long it can stay alight. Flirtation, seduction, commitment, marriage...complacency?

We all know that the one whom we love the most and would dread losing is the last person we should take for granted.

But inevitably we all do.

Once the bond is forged, couples turn as a unit to achieving such things as building a home, raising a family or establishing a business. The expected routines and the regular arrangements facilitate such goals.

The 'slippers existence' to which most of us succumb at one time or another has its own life cycle.

The drop into the routine 'normality' of a consolidated relationship is keenly felt by the women. The period of courtship is a heady one for them— they feel special and revel in the attention.

Men generally welcome how routines take over the marriage as this frees them to get back to their favoured worlds of work and other men.

Indeed, most men abandon courtship when they have accomplished the conquest. Gone are the long, meaningful conversations, the intensity, the romantic walks, the dinners and dates, the flowers, the little gestures, the celebrating of personal rituals and anniversaries.

This spells the death sentence of romance for women.

A woman requires wooing constantly,
or she will dream about
finding it elsewhere.

Yet countless preconceptions, bonds,
a sense of duty and, more often than not,
sheer necessity, keep it just a daydream.

Few married women have the courage or
irresponsibility – depending on one's point
of view – to bolt.

In compensation, many lapse into a world
of fantasy, populated by the heroes of the
day – sundry celebrities whose private antics
can be espied for the price of a tabloid
newspaper...
...or imaginary ones found on the pages of
romantic novels or in the episodes of TV
soap operas.

They flagellate their bodies into shape,
try different diets, buy expensive
creams and make-up.
For if only they could realise their
fantasies, they too would be
worshipped forever after, taken on
dream-like cruises, given small jewel
boxes under the stars and have
sweet nothings
whispered in their ear.

Women who feel neglected do engage in such forms of escapism, but these are doubtless less destructive than drowning their sorrows in alcohol or seeking help in anti-depressants.

The relationship now becomes poisoned with acrimony and recrimination; if the couple stay together it is usually out of habit or fear of being alone. It could then be well nigh impossible to rekindle passion.

Recapturing long gone yearnings requires taking a step back and some imagination.

Seeing your spouse as someone else's lover and looking at him or her through that person's eyes generates a healthy insecurity. It keeps complacency at bay and puts us on our toes.

Yet while it is a cliché to say that we all change in the course of life, it is a truism to point out that people cannot change back to what they were.

People who are able to communicate find lasting pleasure in each other's company and are less likely to forsake that for the dubious delights of an affair.

Lest my views on what sustains long-term relationships appear ambiguous, let me say this:

> *A lasting love match needs to encompass all the ingredients – companionship without lust is but a friendship based on false premises. To shoehorn such a friendship within the framework of a marriage, for example, is to create an artificial constraint.*

Once the children are grown up, and men and women edge towards that undefined crossroad – middle age – the dynamics of a relationship change.

For one thing, many bonds are dismantled. Relative freedom from children, careers – or even previous husbands or wives – means that passion can burn brighter and people can focus on each other with single-minded and intense devotion once again. But this is also the time when, if there is general lassitude and no motivation to try to resuscitate youthful passion, new relationships can take root.

Love and seduction at this stage of life can be reminiscent of the experiences of youth.

The balance is very fragile, however.

Women often show great need for
affection and can be very demanding
and possessive in later years.
This can become an emotional
burden to their man.

At first men relish the shifting of a woman's
emotional dependence until, that is, she
becomes too needy. Women are very fragile
at this point and can easily become a
liability — to themselves, to their families
and to the man they so want.

Men can be vulnerable in
mid-life too. At times, they exhibit a
deplorable lack of judgement in the
pursuit of their vanishing youth.
Their ego can be as fragile as it

once was in their late teens.
The pressure not to show this
fragility or any lack of
confidence is, however, greater.

A woman's sensuality reaches an unsuspected intensity in mid-life. Lavishing it on one man makes sense only if it is fully reciprocated.

A woman of a certain age, who has no direction or interest in life other than her interest in or love for, a man, is exceedingly vulnerable.

Channelling energy into an intellectual pursuit or a challenging project can help her to avoid this; travel and exploring new horizons are liberating.

Such independence often has a desirable side effect in that it tugs at the emotions of a partner who feels secure to the point of complacency.

> *As the years pile up sensuality sharpens precisely because sexual drive slows in pace. Nonetheless, people have the capacity to conceive passion for one another well into old age —and to consummate it, too.*

The eternal question — whether men and women are monogamous or polygamous in their make-up — is constantly re-examined and answered in diametrically opposed ways.

In as much as it is in our nature to strive constantly for exclusivity — because it makes us feel better about ourselves — we are monogamous.

In that we constantly test our desirability